WILDERNESS
SURVIVAL SKILLS

MAKING SHELTER
IN THE WILD

DAVE MACK

PowerKiDS press.

New York

Published in 2016 by The Rosen Publishing Group, Inc.
29 East 21st Street, New York, NY 10010

First Edition

Editor: Sarah Machajewski
Book Design: Michael J. Flynn

Photo Credits: Cover (man) fstop123/E+/Getty Images; cover (shelter in forest) Benjamin Haas/Shutterstock.com; cover, pp. 1, 3–4, 6, 8, 10, 12–14, 16–20, 22–24 (map background) Sergei Drozd/Shutterstock.com; p. 4 Blend Images/Shutterstock.com; p. 5 Max Topchii/Shutterstock.com; p. 7 Phoric/Shutterstock.com; p. 9 © iStockphoto/simongurney; p. 11 David Roth/The Image Bank/Getty Images; p. 12 oliveromg/Shutterstock.com; p. 13 Thinglass/Shutterstock.com; p. 14 Zadiraka Evgenii/Shutterstock.com; p. 15 SF photo/Shutterstock.com; p. 16 Jon Gibbs/Oxford Scientific/Getty Images; p. 17 Photos by R A Kearton/Moment Open/Getty Images; p. 18 Sam Burt Photography/E+/Getty Images; p. 19 @Michi B./Moment/Getty Images; p. 20 Cyndi Monaghan/Moment/Getty Images; p. 21 kanin.studio/Shutterstock.com; p. 22 Bruce Raynor/Shutterstock.com.

Cataloging-in-Publication Data

Names: Mack, Dave L., 1955-.
Title: Making shelter in the wild / Dave Mack.
Description: New York : PowerKids Press, 2016. | Series: Wilderness survival skills | Includes index.
Identifiers: ISBN 9781508143239 (pbk.) | ISBN 9781508143246 (6 pack) | ISBN 9781508143253 (library bound)
Subjects: LCSH: Wilderness survival–Juvenile literature. | Survival–Juvenile literature.
Classification: LCC GV200.5 M33 2016 | DDC 613.6'9–dc23

Manufactured in the United States of America

CPSIA Compliance Information: Batch #BW16PK: For Further Information contact Rosen Publishing, New York, New York at 1-800-237-9932

CONTENTS

A NOTE TO READERS

Always talk with a parent or teacher before proceeding with any of the activities found in this book. Some activities require adult supervision.

A NOTE TO PARENTS AND TEACHERS

READY FOR ANYTHING

Many people love spending time in the **wilderness**. It's fun to camp in the woods or swim in the ocean. Hiking and having outdoor cookouts are other great ways to enjoy nature.

The wilderness can be beautiful and fun. However, it also has **risks**. Why is that? Weather, animals, and your surroundings can be **unpredictable**. But if you spend time preparing, you'll be ready for anything.

You don't have to be an expert wilderness adventurer to enjoy everything nature has to offer—you just have to be willing to face **challenges** if they arise.

THE IMPORTANCE OF BEING PREPARED

Everyone who enters the wilderness must enter prepared. One way to be prepared is to study the **environment** you're going into. Knowing the conditions will let you know what to bring and how to stay safe when you're there.

Another way to be prepared is to have survival skills. A survival skill is anything that helps you stay alive in a dangerous, or unsafe, **situation**. This includes knowing how to build shelter. A shelter is a place that gives **protection** from bad weather or danger.

SURVIVAL TIP

Knowing how to find food and water, make fire, give basic first aid, and read a map are other survival skills you should know.

A few trees and fallen branches can be turned into an acceptable survival shelter.

THE NUMBER-ONE SKILL

Many people think knowing how to build a shelter is the number-one survival skill a person can have. Shelter is important for many reasons. It keeps rain and snow out. It provides shade from the hot sun and protection from strong winds. It hides you from wild animals. Most importantly, shelter keeps you warm.

Everything mentioned above can be found in the wilderness: bad weather, animals, and big **temperature** changes, especially at night. Can you see why it's important to know how to build a survival shelter?

SURVIVAL TIP

Being in very hot or cold weather can lead to dehydration, which is when your body doesn't have enough water. Shelter can help protect you from this.

Successful shelters are **waterproof** and windproof. Staying dry and warm will help you survive.

FACING THE UNEXPECTED

It's unlikely anyone goes into the wilderness thinking they'll have to build a survival shelter. If you're there for a day, you probably won't need it. If you're camping overnight, you'll likely bring a tent. However, you never know what can happen in the wild.

When it comes to the wilderness, you have to expect the unexpected. Something may keep you from exiting the wilderness safely. If you're lost or hurt, it can be better to stay put. Your tent might rip or get lost. In these situations, knowing how to build shelter is important.

SURVIVAL TIP

If something happens to your tent, save what you can. The covering and poles can be used to build a new shelter.

It's a good idea to pack tools that can be used to make shelter. This includes a knife, rope, blanket, and garbage bags or a tarp, which is a large sheet of waterproof cloth or plastic.

STARTING TO BUILD

In a survival situation, your first task should always be to make shelter. First, find somewhere to build it. Look for a flat area with large objects, such as trees or rocks. You can use these objects to support your shelter.

Next, gather building **materials**. Look for big pieces of wood, such as branches and logs. They'll be used for your shelter's frame. Also look for leaves, grass, or pine **boughs**. These materials will cover the shelter's frame.

SURVIVAL TIP

Don't build your shelter in a low-lying area. If it rains, water might collect where you are. Somewhere flat, high, and dry is the best choice.

This tree is a perfect support for building a shelter. It's large, it's heavy, and it won't move.

BUILDING A LEAN-TO

A lean-to is a common survival shelter. It's simple and easy to make. First, find two trees standing close together. Make a beam by tying a log between the trees high off the ground. Use rope if you have it. Vines and woven grass can be used as rope, too.

Once the beam is secure, make a frame of logs or branches. Next, cover it with plant material. You can use a tarp or garbage bags if you have them. You can also stack branches in a line against the beam.

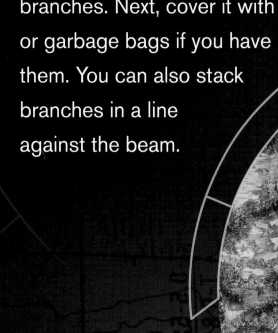

The roof of your lean-to should keep rain and wind out. Cover your frame with grass, leaves, and mud. If you're using a tarp or garbage bags, make sure to tie down the edges so they don't blow away.

SURVIVAL TIP

If there are no trees nearby, create posts for your beam using thick logs or branches.

TEPEES

A tepee, or wikiup, takes more effort to build, but it's a great survival shelter. Gather logs or branches that are about the same length. Use three of them to create a **tripod**, making sure they're secure where they meet. Then, place branches around the tripod.

Next, fill in the empty spaces with plant material. Starting from the bottom, place leaves, grass, and pine boughs in layers until they reach the top. This keeps the inside of the tepee warm and dry.

SURVIVAL TIP

It's possible to keep a fire going inside a tepee as long as it's safely away from anything that could catch on fire. Do not attempt this without an adult's help.

Tepees and lean-tos aren't the only survival shelters. Anything that covers you and keeps you out of the weather counts as shelter.

SHELTERS OF SNOW

Lean-tos and tepees may not be helpful if you need to survive in a cold, snowy environment. Snow caves are a good option in such a place. Snow caves should be small enough so your body heat can keep it warm.

Build a snow cave where there's at least 5 feet (1.5 m) of snow, or shovel the snow into a pile at least that high. Pack the snow until it feels firm. Dig a tunnel through the snow pile, and then clear out the inside to make a small room. The ceiling and sides should be at least 1 foot (0.3 m) thick.

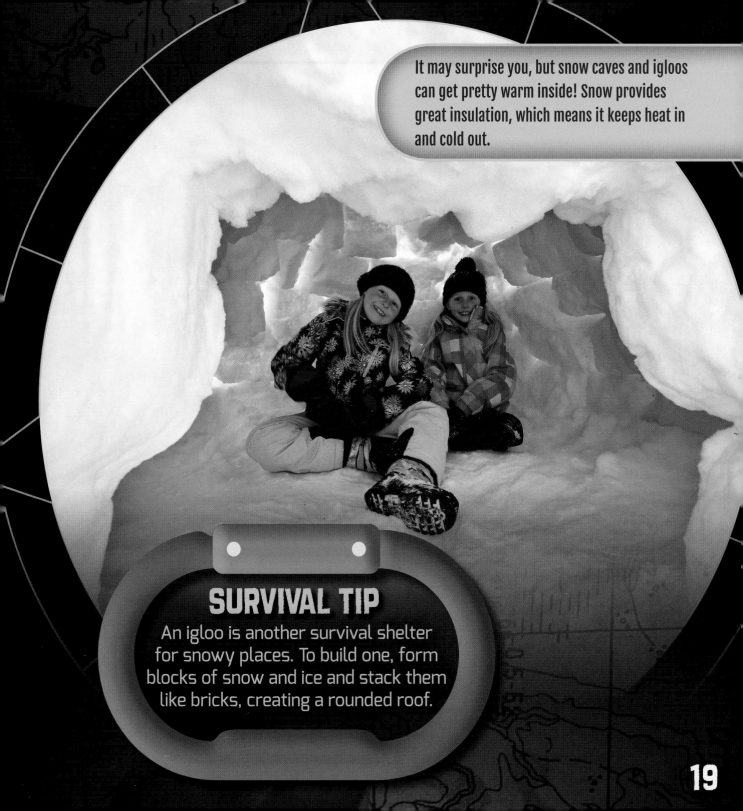

It may surprise you, but snow caves and igloos can get pretty warm inside! Snow provides great insulation, which means it keeps heat in and cold out.

SURVIVAL TIP

An igloo is another survival shelter for snowy places. To build one, form blocks of snow and ice and stack them like bricks, creating a rounded roof.

A FEW MORE TIPS

No matter what kind of survival shelter you build, there are some important tips to keep in mind. Make your shelter as waterproof as possible. Your goal is to stay dry and warm.

Make a sleeping area that's least 6 inches (15 cm) off the ground, because the ground will take in your body heat. You can make a bed out of leaves, pine boughs, or soft sticks. In snow caves and igloos, make the inside roof as smooth and rounded as possible. When the snow melts, the water will run down the sides rather than drip onto you.

Survival Shelter Tips

- If you need to be rescued, mark the entrance to your shelter with bright colors to make it easy to spot. A bright flag or piece of clothing will do.

- A fallen tree can be used to make shelter. Stack branches or logs against the fallen tree, and crawl underneath.

- If you need to stay warm, create a pile of leaves and plants. Crawl in the middle, and cover your body with them to stay warm.

- Building shelter can use a lot of **energy**. Make sure to take breaks, eat, and drink water. You need to save your energy to survive.

- Always go into the wilderness with warm, waterproof clothing. This will help you if your shelter isn't that warm.

- In a pinch, dig a pit in snow, sand, or dirt. Cover the top with a tarp, and you have shelter.

Keep these important tips in mind as you build your survival shelter. The more you practice, the better you'll get at it!

STAY SAFE!

Knowing how to build simple survival shelters will help keep you safe, warm, and dry in any survival situation. This protection will help you survive until you can safely make it out of the wilderness or until a search party finds you.

When you're planning a trip to the wilderness, always keep your safety in mind. Wear the right kind of clothing. Bring light materials that can be used to build shelter in an **emergency**. Always tell someone where you're going. With these tips, your trip to the wilderness will be fun—and safe!

GLOSSARY

bough: A main branch of a tree.

challenge: Something that tests someone's abilities.

emergency: A serious and often dangerous situation that calls for action right away.

energy: The power to do work.

environment: The surroundings in which a person, animal, or plant lives.

material: The matter used to make something.

protection: The act of keeping something safe. "To protect" is "to keep safe."

risk: Something that could put someone in an unsafe situation.

situation: A series of events in which a person finds themself.

temperature: How hot or cold something is.

tripod: A three-legged structure used for support.

unpredictable: Not able to be expected or known in advance.

waterproof: Able to keep water out.

wilderness: A natural, wild place.

INDEX

WEBSITES

Due to the changing nature of Internet links, PowerKids Press has developed an online list of websites related to the subject of this book. This site is updated regularly. Please use this link to access the list: www.powerkidslinks.com/wss/she/